CBT Workbook for Teens

Manage to Find Relief from Anxiety, Panic Attack, Negative Thinking and Unwanted Thoughts

By

B. Smith

MHS Publishers

© **Copyright 2022 by MHS Publishers- All rights reserved.**

Without the prior written permission of the Publisher, no part of this publication may be stored in a retrieval system, replicated, or transferred in any form or medium, digital, scanning, recording, printing, mechanical, or otherwise, except as permitted under 1976 United States Copyright Act, section 107 or 108. Permission concerns should be directed to the Publisher's permission department.

Legal Notice

This book is copyright protected. It is only to be used for personal purposes. Without the author's or Publisher's permission, you cannot paraphrase, quote, copy, distribute, sell, or change any part of the information in this book.

Disclaimer Notice

This book is written and published independently. Please keep in mind that the material in this publication is solely for educational and entertaining purposes. All efforts have provided authentic, up-to-date, trustworthy, and comprehensive information. There are no express or implied assurances. The purpose of this book's material is to assist readers in having a better understanding of the subject matter. The activities, information, and exercises are provided solely for self-help information. This book is not intended to replace expert psychologists, legal, financial, or other guidance. If you require counseling, please get in touch with a qualified professional.

By reading this text, the reader accepts that the author will not be held liable for any damages, indirectly or directly, experienced due to the information included herein, particularly, but not limited to, omissions, errors, or inaccuracies. You are accountable for your decisions, actions, and consequences as a reader.

About the Author

B. Smith is a certified psychologist and does private practice. She also teaches psychology. She has recently worked with young people with acute anxiety in an intensive cognitive behavioral therapy (CBT) program. She is specialized in cognitive behavioral therapy (CBT) for depression, OCD, and anxiety disorders in children, adolescents, and adults. After working with several teenagers who were utterly oblivious to what was happening to them, Smith concluded that teenagers who experience anxiety and panic attacks frequently tend to ignore it or are unable to receive therapy. She has written this book with worksheets so readers could help themselves, outlining the issues and providing solutions.

Table of Contents

About the Author 3

Introduction 6

Chapter 1: Cognitive Behavioral Therapy (CBT) 8

   1.1 What Is CBT? 8

   1.2 How Will It Help Me? 9

   1.3   How Effective Is This Method? 10

   1.4 CBT With Anxiety, Panic Attacks, And Negative, Unwanted Thinking 12

Chapter 2: Overcoming Anxiety With CBT And Worksheets. 14

   2.1 Do I Have Anxiety? 14

   2.2   Anxiety Recognition Questions 18

   2.3   Symptoms Checklist 22

   2.4   My Triggers Worksheet 24

   2.5   Breaking Down My Thoughts 26

   2.6 Finding My Own Coping Methods 29

   2.7 Preparing For Anxiety 32

Chapter 3: Fighting A Panic Attack With CBT Worksheets 34

   3.1 Understanding A Panic Attack 34

   3.2 Behavior Analysis Worksheet 37

   3.3 My Triggers 39

   3.4 Exercises To Help Calm Down 42

   3.5 Panic Attack Record Sheet And Crisis Plan 48

Chapter 4: Stopping Negative Thinking And Unwanted Thoughts With CBT And Worksheets 51
   4.1 Unhelpful Thinking 51
   4.2 Reality Acceptance Activities.................................... 54
   4.3 Challenging Negative Thoughts Questionnaire 55
   4.4 Brain Dump List 58
   4.5 Self Affirmations.. 61

Chapter 5: Activities To Stop Me From Feeling Anxious.......... 62
   5.1 30-Day Anxiety Challenge 62
   5.2 Anxiety Reduction Exercises 63
   5.3 I-Statements.. 64
   5.4 Getting Over Negative Thinking Games and Activities 65
   5.5 How do I Feel? 68
   5.6 Brain Dump Journal... 69

Conclusion.. 70

Introduction

Adolescents frequently experience dread and worry as a regular part of growing up, but when these feelings overwhelm kids and begin to interfere with their everyday life. It is more than just worry; it is a sign of anxiety. Teenagers experience anxiety so frequently and intensely that they become uneasy. It starts to interfere with their daily lives. They find themselves forgoing activities like using the elevator or arriving late to class because they are so afraid that something terrible will happen. They would believe it would be life-threatening and experience an extremely intense reaction like a panic attack. They stop doing simple things because they fear harm, dangerous, or even fatal results. As a result, they begin to avoid dealing with such situations altogether, disrupting their day-to-day activities at school, home, and interpersonal relationships with friends.

More than 32% of teens experience anxiety, and even though therapy can effectively treat anxiety, more than half go undiagnosed and untreated. According to research, CBT is the best method for treating anxiety since it works the best for Teens. CBT has a 50–75% success rate in treating depression and anxiety when used alone. In addition, it has the most proof that it helps persons with Generalized Anxiety Disorder (GAD), panic disorder, specific phobias, and social anxiety disorder to lessen their symptoms. The CBT-inspired activities in this book will make you more conscious of your feelings and thoughts and allows you to manage your anxiety, panic attacks, and negative thoughts in various healthier, more effective ways. You may manage your anxiety and prevent it from taking over your life by using the CBT worksheets and other activities in this book to help you identify triggers, coping techniques, and much more.

School and parental pressure, peer pressure, social media pressure, fear, and other legitimate causes of anxiety can all be overcome because they are all mental and are brought on by worrying excessively about potential outcomes like disappointing your parents, getting hurt, or even dying. However, you are not in danger in most cases, and the worry is all in your mind. CBT helps you realize that and mentally process that through these worksheets.

The book includes a questionnaire to help you recognize the type of anxiety, panic attacks and negative thing you have. Finding all the symptoms you get while experiencing anxiety attacks through a checklist is a crucial step to help you discover the triggers of these attacks. Once you find out the problem, you can easily find a solution and ways to cope and react to it effectively when you go through the same things again. The book has it all and acts like your companion and guide to a happy life.

Chapter 1: Cognitive Behavioral Therapy (CBT)

CBT is a psychological treatment that teaches patients how to recognize and alter the damaging or unsettling thought patterns that can harm their behavior and moods.

1.1 What Is CBT?

CBT is not limited to recognizing thinking patterns; another goal of CBT is to assist people in overcoming these tendencies. It employs a variety of tactics. Through CBT, false beliefs are exposed, refuted, and replaced with more accurate, realistic beliefs. It is critical to understand the conditions, emotions, and thoughts that lead to actions that prevent people from adapting, adjusting, or participating in different aspects of life.

However, this procedure might be challenging, particularly for those who have trouble examining their thoughts and emotions. But spending the time to name these ideas can also result in self-discovery and offer perceptions vital to the healing procedure.

In cognitive behavioral therapy, people are frequently given new abilities they can use in everyday life. For instance, a person with social anxiety might put new coping mechanisms to the test and practice avoiding or handling social situations positively that might otherwise lead to panic attacks.

During cognitive behavioral therapy, you can learn problem-solving techniques that can help you recognize and address potential issues that could result from both major and minor life stressors. Additionally, it can lessen the harmful effects of both mental and physical sickness. There are five steps to resolving issues.

1. Determine the issue.
2. Make a list of potential answers.
3. Analyze the benefits and drawbacks of each prospective fix.
4. Select a course of action.
5. Use the coping mechanisms and follow through

Setting goals can also help you make changes to enhance your health and quality of life as you recover from mental illness. This involves identifying your goal or distinguishing between short and long-term goals. It also includes helping you focus on the process as much as the end outcome, and it will help you self-monitor throughout and notice your progress and change of thought pattern.

1.2 How Will It Help Me?

The essential ideology of CBT is that thoughts and feelings significantly impact behavior. For instance, someone constantly worried about a lift falling, being trapped in an elevator, and other elevator mishaps, would decide not to use the elevator. Short-term cognitive behavioral therapy can teach patients how to concentrate on their current thoughts and beliefs. Even though they cannot control every part of their environment, they can still control how they perceive and respond to it, like telling them that the chances of getting trapped in an elevator are one in a thousand. Even if it occurs, there will be no harm brought to them.

It aids in developing healthier mental processes by making you aware of the negative and frequently irrational thoughts that negatively affect your feelings and mood and enable you to reason. The development of coping skills that patients can employ now and in the future is one of the cognitive behavioral therapy's most significant advantages. Through CBT, they recognize their triggers and manage to overcome them through coping mechanisms, which helps in the long term.

The treatment for anxiety disorders that is most frequently utilized is cognitive behavioral therapy (CBT). According to research, it is the most helpful in treating various mental illnesses, including panic disorders, social anxiety disorder(SAD), and general anxiety disorder (GAD). The book will serve as a coach during this process, providing you with practical techniques. For instance, you might frequently assume that either everything is evil or everything is perfect. You would substitute the more accurate view that there are numerous Grey areas in between those thoughts. Utilizing these tactics requires practice. You can learn to use the coping mechanisms through CBT to control fear, panic, and anxiety after understanding your anxiety and understanding your anxiety and triggers.

1.3   How Effective Is This Method?

One of the treatment modalities that has undergone the most research nowadays is cognitive behavioral therapy. In addition, numerous mental health issues, such as anxiety, depression, eating disorders, insomnia, obsessive-compulsive disorder, panic disorder, and post-traumatic stress disorder, have all been proven to respond well.

Research has shown that cognitive behavioral therapy is beneficial in addressing the signs and symptoms of depression and anxiety in children and adolescents. People with anxiety and problems related to anxiety reported seeing better results from CBT. It helps patients gain better self-control, avoid triggers, and create coping mechanisms for everyday stressors.

You must be prepared and eager to put in the time and effort necessary to thoroughly examine your thoughts and feelings for cognitive behavioral therapy to be effective. Although self-analysis can be challenging, it is an excellent approach to understanding how our interior states influence our actions on the outside. CBT often involves a progressive procedure that aids little effort toward behavior modification. For instance, a person with social anxiety may begin by merely visualizing social settings that make them anxious. They could then practice speaking with friends, relatives, and strangers. The process appears less complicated, and the goals are more doable as you gradually work toward a more significant objective.

CBT can help people with the panic disorder find practical techniques to control their symptoms. A person can learn to effectively manage their symptoms even if they may not be able to handle them when they experience a panic attack. CBT uses a two-step method to help the client make a long-lasting transformation. A variety of exercises and activities to teach the client how to recognize their negative ideas and how to substitute them with more constructive ones

1.4 CBT With Anxiety, Panic Attacks, And Negative, Unwanted Thinking

Anxiety affects 31% of teenagers between the ages of 13 and 18 every year. People who suffer from anxiety may attempt to control their reactions by avoiding triggers since they typically respond to negative thinking, emotions, and circumstances more greatly. Sadly, this kind of avoidance just serves to amplify worries and fears. To assist you in controlling your anxiety, the majority of current therapy approaches focus on avoidance and negative thinking. Cognitive behavioral therapy (CBT) aims to recognize and comprehend your negative thought patterns and inefficient behavior patterns and replace them with more sensible ideas, practical activities, and coping mechanisms.

Years of research have demonstrated that CBT successfully treats anxiety problems. Because it has the most proof that it works for people with Generalized Anxiety Disorder (GAD), panic disorder, specific phobias, and Social Anxiety Disorder (SAD), CBT is regarded as the "gold standard" treatment for anxiety disorders. Exposure therapy involves facing feared situations that typically cause a significant reaction, leading to a dramatic decrease in symptoms as they start to visualize that the situation might not be as bad.

Professionals who treat panic disorder tend to favor CBT over other forms of therapy due to its shown efficacy, goal-oriented emphasis, and speedy outcomes. Helping clients break free from harmful thought patterns so they can make better decisions about their actions and behaviors is one of the critical objectives of CBT. Generally speaking, those with panic disorder are more likely to be subject to pessimistic ideas and self-defeating attitudes, which can impair self-esteem and exacerbate anxiety. Panic attacks, the primary symptom of panic disorder, are frequently accompanied by fearful and pessimistic thoughts. In addition, physical and mental symptoms are typically present during panic attacks. These symptoms can trigger upsetting thoughts like a fear of losing control, going insane, or dying because they are frequently seen as terrifying. Cognitive behavioral therapy (CBT) effectively manages anxiety and panic attacks through activities and exercises. These activities and exercises teach you to become aware of your negative thoughts and replace them with healthier ways of thinking. They also help to build healthy coping mechanisms to alter maladaptive behaviors, cognitive behavioral therapy (CBT) assists in effectively managing anxiety and panic attacks. Using relaxation techniques also aids in lowering stress, controlling anxiety, and surviving panic episodes.

Chapter 2: Overcoming Anxiety with CBT and Worksheets

It is normal and common to worry about an exam coming or an interview since those are rare and important steps in our lives. Still, when excess worry starts taking place, it becomes an anxiety disorder problem. Therefore, finding triggers and coping methods through effective ways to tackle anxiety like CBT worksheets, is essential.

2.1 Do I Have Anxiety?

Those with anxiety disorders frequently stress and worry excessively about everyday situations. Recurrent occurrences of severe anxiousness are a symptom of several anxiety disorders.

The following list includes anxiety symptoms and warning signs:

- Experiencing tension, annoyance, or discomfort
- A sense of imminent danger, anxiety, or hopelessness
- An accelerated heartbeat
- Rapid panting (hyperventilation)
- Perspiring
- Quaking
- Feeling exhausted or weak
- Having trouble concentrating or worrying about everything but the present situation
- Having difficulty getting to sleep
- Digestive system problems
- Having issues controlling worry

But do you have an anxiety disorder, or is it just regular worry? Here is a way to differentiate. This assessment is to see if you have symptoms common in people with an anxiety disorder.

Which Is it?

Everyday Anxiety	Anxiety Disorder
Anxiety over paying bills, getting jobs, ending a relationship, or other significant life events	Worry that is persistent and unabated results in severe distress and interferes with daily living.
Self-consciousness or embarrassment in an uncomfortable or awkward circumstance	Avoiding social settings because of a fear of humiliation or embarrassment
An instance of anxiety or sweating before a significant test, business presentation, or other important events	Experiencing sudden panic attacks and obsessing about the dread of suffering another one
Realistic apprehensions about hazardous environments and objects	Irrational aversion to or avoidance of something that presents little to no threat to you
Immediately after a stressful occurrence, anxiety, grief, or difficulty sleeping may occur.	Dreams and flashbacks that keep coming back to a horrible experience that happened months or years ago

Do I Have An Anxiety Disorder?

Use this checklist to identify your symptoms over the past three months. Share your completed list with your doctor or mental health professional to support your assessment.

- [ ] I tend to worry more than others
- [ ] I feel agitated or on-edge
- [ ] I feel restless, like I need to move
- [ ] I am fatigued
- [ ] I have difficulty concentrating
- [ ] I can be irritable
- [ ] I have tense muscles
- [ ] I have trouble falling or staying asleep
- [ ] I experience panic attacks
- [ ] I avoid social situations
- [ ] I have a phobia

2.2 Anxiety Recognition Questions

It is essential to recognize your type of anxiety, whether it is social anxiety, generalized anxiety disorder, or panic disorder.

There are numerous varieties of anxiety, such as:

- Agoraphobia is an anxiety disorder in which a person fears and frequently avoids locations or situations that can make them feel confined, helpless, or ashamed.
- Anxiety and worry about common or routine things, as well as persistent and excessive tension, are symptoms of generalized anxiety disorder. The fear is disproportionate to the situation and impacts how you physically feel. It frequently co-occurs with depression or other anxiety disorders.
- High degrees of anxiety, fear, and avoidance of social situations are symptoms of a social anxiety disorder (social phobia), which are brought on by emotions of humiliation, self-consciousness, and worry about being judged or perceived adversely by others.

Here's a quick way to Calm Your Mind & Release Stress

INHALE 3...2...1

breathe

DEEP BREATH IN

HOLD 1...2...3

HOLD 1...2...3

DEEP BREATH OUT

INHALE 3...2...1

Social anxiety is a disorder characterized by overwhelming anxiety or self-consciousness in ordinary social situations to milder cases, the symptoms of social anxiety only appear in specific situations, such as public speaking. On the more extreme end, any form of social interaction can act as a trigger

Because everyone's thoughts, feelings, and reactions to social anxiety are different, it's valuable to spend some time thinking about your unique experience.

Which social situations are you anxious about?

Giving a speech	Spending time alone with a friend	Going on a date	Attending a crowded
Going to the grocery store	Making eye contact	Being the center of attention	Talking on the phone
Meeting someone new	Dealing with authority figures	_____	_____

What are you worried about during social situations?

Embarrassing myself	Looking stupid	My physical appearance	Being disliked
Being rejected	Not knowing what to talk about	Being noticed	_____

Oftentimes, social anxiety will lead a person to build their life in a "safe" way that shields them from their fears, rather than living how they truly want. This is a form of avoidance, which will actually make anxiety worse over time. Next, we'll explore how social anxiety and avoidance has impacted your life.

List three ways in which social anxiety has impacted your life. For example, did anxiety affect your choice of career? Has it affected your relationships?

1	
2	
3	

Imagine you wake up tomorrow, and your social anxiety is gone. How would your life be different? List three examples, being an specific as possible.

1	
2	
3	

This assessment will help you recognize if you have social anxiety. If you think that only a few of these are relatable, then it is likely you do not have social anxiety but some other kind of anxiety. In that case, here is another type of assessment. If you can answer all these questions, you will be able to recognize your type of anxiety.

Anxiety Questions
Answer these questions to explore your anxiety!

What would things look like if you were able to cope with your anxiety?

What's the worst you're ever felt because of your anxiety?

What are your top five anxiety triggers?

Can you tell me about a time you handled your anxiety in a healthy way?

How do your family members cope with their anxiety?

What do you need to hear from others when you're feeling anxious?

How has your anxiety impacted your relationships with others?

What happens to your body when you start to feel anxious?

What do you need others to do when you're anxious?

Do you think you'll ever be able to cope with your anxiety?

How do you think your anxiety could impact you in the future?

What are some things that your anxiety has kept you from doing?

When is your anxiety at its worst?

What are some other feelings you experience when you're anxious?

What does your anxiety look like at home, school, or in the neighborhood?

What things make your anxiety worse?

What kind of thoughts go through head when you're anxious?

2.3 Symptoms Checklist

Knowing what symptoms, you have when you experience anxiety or anxiety attacks is essential to find cures and coping methods effectively. Tick the options that affect you regularly.

Anxiety Symptoms Checklist

☐	My heart beat really fast	☐	I have thoughts of death or dying
☐	I feel afraid	☐	My skin feels cold and damp
☐	My skin feels warm/hot	☐	I have trouble sitting still
☐	I have thoughts of things going wrong	☐	I have trouble breathing
☐	My voice trembles	☐	I feel like I'm losing control
☐	I have trouble falling or staying asleep	☐	I start to worry about everything
☐	I get a headache or stomachache	☐	I feel nauseous or sick
☐	I feel like running away	☐	I get really jumpy or "on edge"
☐	My mind starts racing	☐	I start to sweat
☐	I avoid being around certain people	☐	I feel exhausted
☐	I feel like I'm going crazy	☐	My chest starts to feel tight
☐	Little things start to irritate me	☐	My muscles get tense
☐	I feel like being left alone	☐	I have trouble relaxing
☐	I have a hard time talking to others	☐	I avoid going certain places
☐	I feel out of control or helpless	☐	I start feeling depressed
☐	I lose focus easily and can't concentrate	☐	I get a "lump" in my throat
☐	I start to shake	☐	My fingers or toes start to tingle
☐	I lose my appetite	☐	I use the bathroom more frequently

How Anxiety Feels in My Body

Color in the feelings you have in your body when you feel anxious.

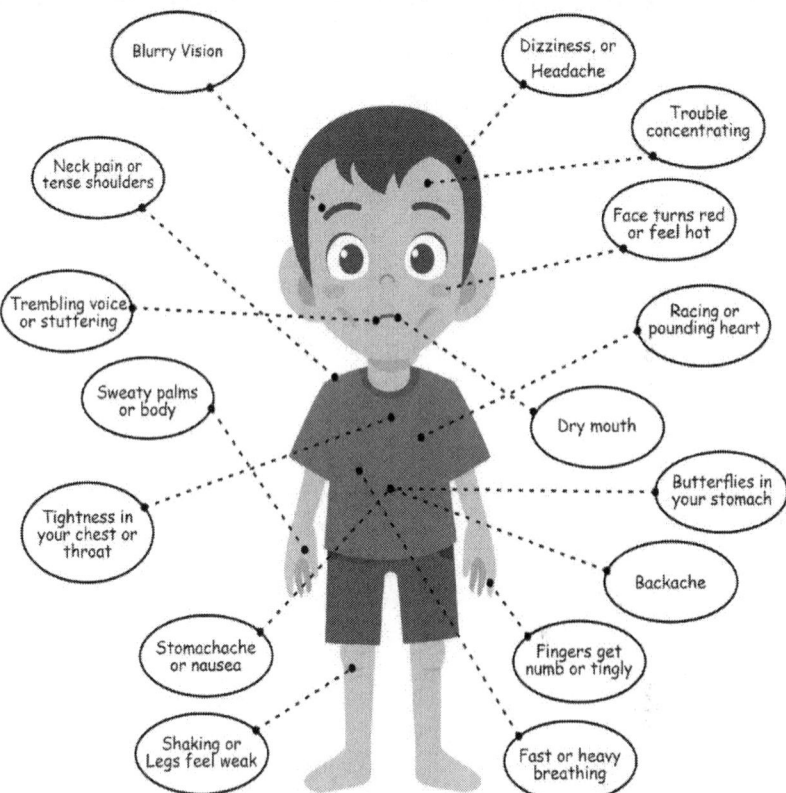

What other symptoms do you experience when you are anxious?

_____
_____
_____
_____

2.4 My Triggers Worksheet

It is critical to identify the sources of your anxiety. Understanding the root of your anxiety can help you better control it. Although anxiety causes might vary from person to person, many of them are shared by those with these problems. Most people discover that they have several triggers. However, anxiety attacks can occur for no apparent reason in some people. Therefore, it is crucial to identify any anxiety triggers you may have. The first step in managing your triggers is to recognize them.

Note the times your anxiety is pronounced and any potential triggers you can think of. And then, compare it to the list, marking off each trigger you believe impacted you.

Anxiety Triggers

An anxiety trigger is something that happens to make you feel anxious or nervous. Go through this list and on an a scale of 1-10, identify how anxious each of the triggers makes you feel.

1	2	3	4	5	6	7	8	9	10

CALM   A LITTLE ANXIOUS   ANXIOUS   EXTREMELY ANXIOUS!

____ Conflict or drama in relationships

____ Being in a large crowd of people

____ Meeting new people

____ Going to a new place for the first time

____ Having to confront someone

____ Interacting on social media

____ Having too much to do

____ Giving a presentation in front of the class

____ Working as part of a group

____ Pressure to act or behave a certain way

____ Performing in front of other people

____ Things not going the way I planned

____ Having to change up my routine

____ Grades or stress from schoolwork

____ Having too much time by my self

____ Being away from my phone for too long

____ Friends not texting me back

____ Loud noises or raised voices

____ Other people being disappointed in me

____ Watching the news

____ Having conversations with peers or adults

____ Not feeling prepared

____ Being in tight spaces, like an elevator

____ Being in wide open spaces

____ Being around certain people

____ Interacting with someone I have a crush on

____ Not knowing what is going to happen

____ Not having enough money

____ Not knowing what career I want to have

____ School violence

____ Family stress (divorce, finances, etc..)

____ A sick friends or family member

____ Rumors about me spreading around school

____ My job, boss, or co-workers

____ Other people's expectations of me

____ Thinking about college

____ Having to be the one to make decisions

____ Making new friends

____ Changes in my body or my weight

____ Interacting with a certain family member

____ Feeling left out by my peer group

____ Become an adult with more responsibilities

What are some other things that make you feel anxious?

2.5 Breaking Down My Thoughts

Accepting that not all intrusive thoughts indicate a valid reason to worry is one technique to deal with anxiety. Simply put, not all beliefs are true. Therefore, attempting to refute the ideas is frequently fruitless. Instead, try an acceptance-based strategy. In an acceptance-based approach, you simply observe the thought you are thinking without feeling compelled to address, correct, refute, or even believe it. You are not concentrating on it, just allowing it to pass and go.

Fear (what are you frightened of right now?)	Fact (rational counterpart to this fear, what is actually true? What is there evidence of?)
1.	1.
2.	2.
3.	3.
4.	4.
5.	5.

Another way you can challenge anxiety is by questioning it. And finally, by not running away and facing it.

De-Catastrophizing

What could I do to solve this problem instead of worrying?

_____
_____
_____

Am I ignoring other factors in the situation which suggest that things will not be as bad as I am predicting?

_____
_____
_____

What could be a more balanced and realistic way of looking at this?

_____
_____
_____

Anxiety Buster
WORKSHEET

TOP STRESSES **WHAT CAN BE DONE?**

Pay attention to "what its" Ask yourself "what is" instead of worrying about imagined scenarios if there's nothing to be done worrying won't help.

_____   _____

_____   _____

_____   _____

_____   _____

TO DO: Write everything swirling in your mind. Seeing it on paper helps things seem more manageable.

_____   _____

_____   _____

_____   _____

_____   _____

TOP 3 PRIORITIES TODAY: Instead of trying to do it all pick 3. Accomplishment increases dopamine!

01. _____   02. _____   03. _____

2.6 Finding My Own Coping Methods

Several quick natural cures could assist you in taking control of the issue if your anxiety is intermittent and interfering with your ability to concentrate or complete chores.

If your anxiety is situation-specific, such as worrying about an upcoming event, you may notice that the feelings are transient and typically go away after the scheduled event.

There are methods you can employ if you fight anxiety to stop feeling overwhelmed by it. There are short-term fixes to help you deal with the situation immediately and long-term strategies to prevent a repeating problem.

- Momentary coping methods
- Breathing Exercises

Do you ever feel like your heart is thumping quicker when under pressure? Perhaps when you are faced with challenging work or occasion, your palms start to sweat. In such situations, use this breathing technique.

- Writing down your thoughts helps you untangle your head and calm down. Likewise, writing down things helps by getting negative things out of your head.
- Long-term coping methods

Try out these many activities, find out which is most effective for you, and circle the one you like the most.

1. Reading empowering books

For those with Anxiety, reading reduces stress by 68%, making it a very highly beneficial activity.

2. Go for walks

Being physically active is crucial for controlling anxiety because it helps the body release surplus energy that otherwise causes anxiety and endorphins. These substances naturally make us feel happy.

3. Cook Healthy Meals

Finding nutritious recipes and experimenting in the kitchen can help you eat more healthfully long-term, significantly reduce your anxiety, and serve as a diversion from your worries.

4. Get Creative

Adult coloring pages, canvas painting, and crossword puzzles are fantastic stress relievers.

5. Connect with animals

Being around animals and petting them can be an excellent activity for anxiety management because they reduce feelings of loneliness and make you happier.

6. Dance by yourself

Another excellent hobby for alleviating tension and anxiety is dancing by yourself when no one is looking.

7. Watch inspiring movies

It can be incredibly uplifting and motivating to change your negative outlook on life by watching inspirational movies, documentaries, or movies based on real life.

8. Do yoga

An effective old method for reducing anxiety is yoga. Yoga can help to alleviate all of the symptoms and misery associated with anxiety, which include making you tighten up, irritable, and rigid.

2.7 Preparing for Anxiety

Signs Anxiety May Be Setting In

- Appears "zoned out" or spacy
- More snappy than normal
- Become more Impatient
- Sturggling to make eye contact
- An increase in avoidance behaviors
- Needing more reassurance
- Struggling to sit still
- Avoid making plans for the future
- Cancels late
- Want to leave early
- Irritable or becomes easily angered

Recognizing the signs that occur when anxiety starts setting in is essential. If you feel these behaviors occur, then know it is a situation where you must prepare yourself.

When it is time for anxiety, and you have recognized your symptoms, triggers and coping methods, it is time to put them into action and face those problems. When you are going into a situation that might make you feel anxious or nervous, it can be helpful to man tally prepare ahead of time. Use this worksheet to think of ways to prepare and cope with the situation. It is essential to face the problem instead of running away from it.

What situation or triggers might make me feel anxious

How have I handled it before

Warning signs that let me know I'm getting anxious

What can I say or do before to prepare for the situation

Coping skills I can use if I start feeling anxious

Chapter 3: Fighting A Panic Attack with CBT Worksheets

Throughout most cases, people only have one or two panic attacks in their lifetimes, and the problem typically disappears once a stressful circumstance is ended. However, you may have panic disorder if you frequently get unplanned panic attacks and endure extended periods of continual worry about having a seizure.

3.1 Understanding A Panic Attack

Even if panic attacks do not pose a life-threatening threat, they can nonetheless be terrifying and substantially influence your quality of life. However, treatment is often highly successful. One of the worst things about them is the crippling fear that you will have another panic attack. You may avoid situations where a panic attack might occur because you are so frightened of getting one. You can be so afraid of experiencing panic attacks that you steer clear of circumstances where they might happen. You might believe you are losing control, experiencing a heart attack, or even going to pass away when panic attacks strike. Typically, panic episodes start abruptly and without warning. They can happen anytime you drive, at the mall, fast asleep, or even in the middle of a work meeting. You could experience panic episodes infrequently or regularly.

The brain instructs the autonomic nervous system to initiate the "flight-or-fight" response when the body is in immediate danger. Numerous substances, including adrenaline, overflow the body and cause physiological changes. For instance, the heart rate, respiration, and blood flow are all increased to prepare for physical fighting or fleeing.

When the "flight-or-fight" reaction is elicited, but there is no real danger, it is believed that a panic attack will develop. A panic attack can appear while seemingly stress-free activities like watching television or falling asleep.

Panic attacks and panic disorders can impact almost every aspect of your life if left untreated. Complications that panic attacks may result in or be related to include:

- The emergence of specific phobias, such as a dread of driving or emigrating
- Regular medical attention for medical disorders and health issues
- Avoiding social interactions
- Issues in the office or school
- Other psychiatric problems include depression, anxiety, and others.
- Suicidal behavior or ideas are more likely to occur
- Abuse of other drugs or alcohol
- Financial difficulties

There are numerous different therapies available for treating panic disorder. However, research indicates that CBT consistently outperforms Applied Relaxation Training (ART) and Panic-Focused Psychodynamic Psychotherapy (PFPP) in treating panic disorder.

Frequently CBT is favored over other forms of therapy due to its shown efficacy, goal-oriented emphasis, and speedy outcomes. CBT enables you to comprehend how your perception of someone else's symptoms impacts your own experience. For example, anxiety symptoms can create a feedback loop by extending and intensifying the "fight or flight" response and maintaining the duration and severity of the panic attack. On the other hand, resisting these ideas can help you regulate your panic and agoraphobia.

Exercises that cause these symptoms are used as a teaching and mastery aid. It will involve journaling, identifying triggers, and developing coping mechanisms.

3.2 Behavior Analysis Worksheet

Many people with panic disorder describe feeling as though they have a heart attack or are on the verge of dying and experiencing some or all of the following symptoms.

SIGNS OF A PANIC ATTACK

- Sweating
- Dizziness
- Accelerated Heart Rate
- Trembling
- Senation of Smothering
- Chest Pain or Discomfort
- Nausea or Abdominal Distress
- Chills or Heat Sensations
- Feeling Dizzy, Unsteady or Faint
- Fear of Losing Control or Dying

Now try and recall the last time you had a panic attack and write down the situation, physical and emotional symptoms and how you responded. Then finally, think of the consequences your actions had. You can track your progress, explore your emotions, and manage your feelings of stress.

Behaviour Analysis

Situation _____

_____

Organism

→ Thoughts _____

_____

→ Emotions _____

_____

→ Body _____

_____

Response (behaviour) _____

_____

_____

_____

Consequences

Short - term _____

Long - term _____

3.3 My Triggers

You are probably all too acquainted with the trembling, shortness of breath, and sense of impending doom if you have ever experienced a panic attack. Understanding the factors that cause severe episodes might help people with panic disorder manage their condition. In addition, it may help you to learn the best coping mechanisms for dealing with their condition.

It can be challenging to pinpoint what causes panic episodes. In addition, it might be challenging to control your symptoms because a panic attack can happen for no apparent reason. Therefore, it is crucial to recognize any triggers you may have. These triggers are not an outcome of a single event but an unresolved long-term issue.

- **Stress**

For a good reason, stress is listed as the leading trigger of panic attacks in the top 10. It is challenging to prevent stress because various factors can bring it on. Stress may be caused by multiple factors, including work, school, family, and health.

- Memories of horrific events

If you have ever gone through a traumatic event, there is a reasonable probability that you will have trouble with anything that can trigger a memory. Panic attacks can occur when one encounters highly unsettling or traumatizing circumstances

- **Social occasions**

While we all occasionally experience social anxiety, social disorder normally affects certain people. You could get overwhelming feelings when there is a lot of noise or a vast number of people around you. An anxiety attack may be brought on by situations requiring social contact or meeting new people. Financial anxiety brought in by Concerns about debt, bills, and finances quickly brought on anxiety.

- **Conflicts or disputes**

A significant disagreement or a tight connection with a loved one frequently causes panic attacks. Conflicts can be particularly distressing because a resolution requires your participation. Additionally, you often depend on the other party to reach an understanding or make reparations, which could give you the impression that you do not have complete control over the circumstance.

Write down the possible triggers you think affected you and caused panic attacks and why that was the case.

What Was The Cause?

1. _____

2. _____

3. _____

4. _____

5. _____

Why Do You Think?

1. _____

2. _____

3. _____

4. _____

5. _____

3.4 Exercises to Help Calm Down

Although there is no miracle cure for panic attacks, you can reduce their length and intensity. So the next time you get a panic attack, take the following actions.

How to Survive a Panic Attack

- **focus on your breathing** — hyperventilating makes your symptoms worse
- **relax your body** — muscle tension makes it harder for your body to expel stress hormones
- **recognise that you're having a panic attack** — you are not dying, or going crazy, this feeling will pass
- **remember** that a panic attack always ends, it usually lasts 10-30 minutes
- **distract your senses** — touch something soft, smell something nice, look at something that makes you happy, listen to
- **don't be afraid to get professional help** if you experience debilitating and recurring attacks

COLOUR Breathing

Color breathing a form of meditation is a good way to reduce stress.

1

Imagine a color. Any color. Yellow, green, red, purple, blue, pink, black, white, orange

2

On your inhale, imagine this color entering your lungs and your body. The color is filing you up. Breathe this color in deeply for a count of three.

3

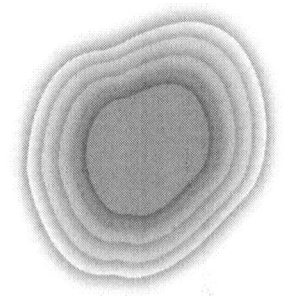

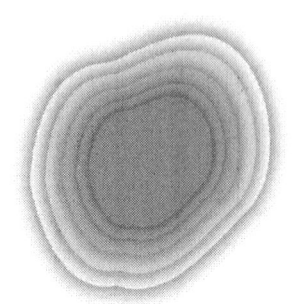

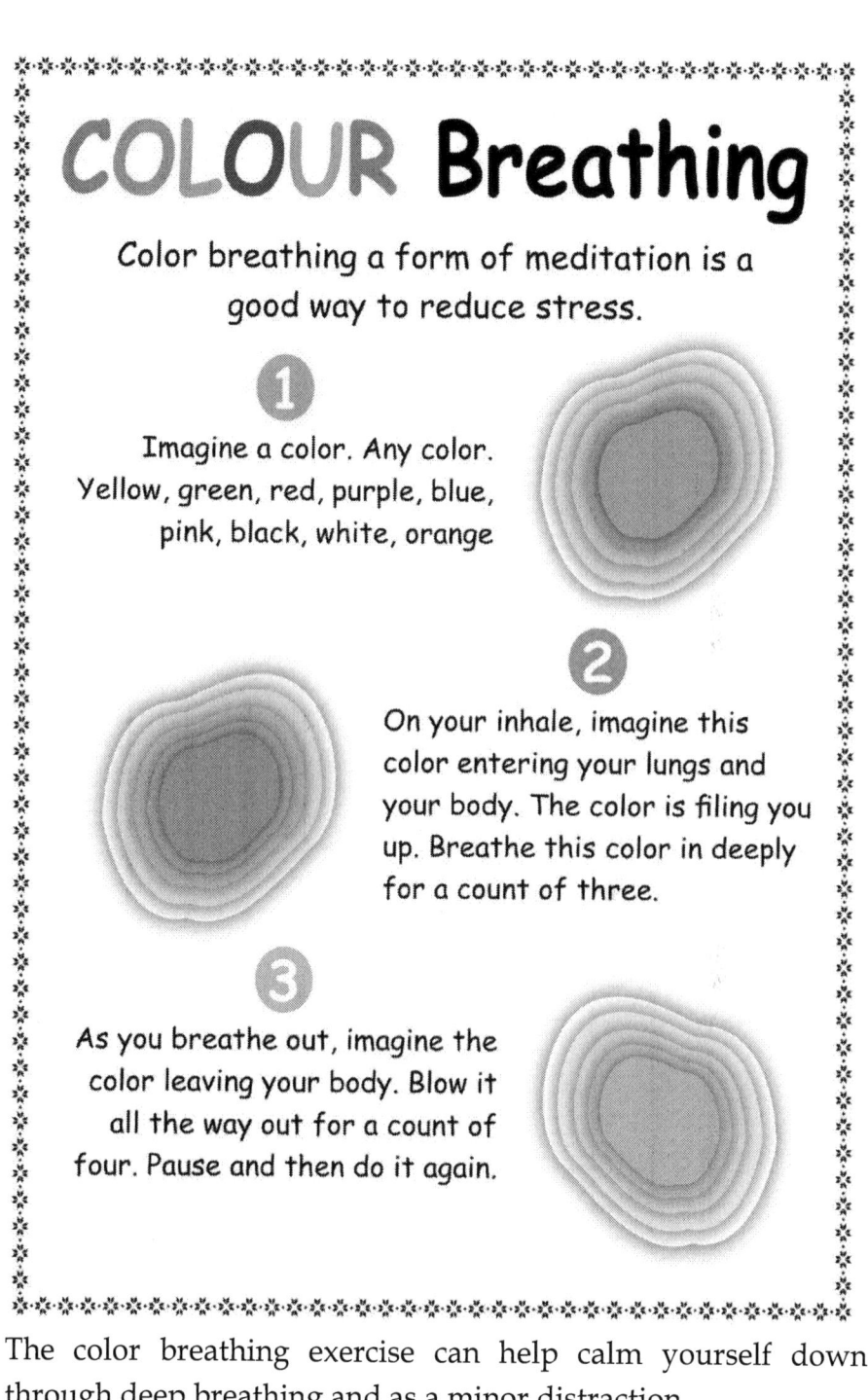

As you breathe out, imagine the color leaving your body. Blow it all the way out for a count of four. Pause and then do it again.

The color breathing exercise can help calm yourself down through deep breathing and as a minor distraction.

There are many other ways to slow your heartbeat and calm down during a panic attack. Next time you experience a panic attack, try the following and then circle the things that were most effective for you. This will help you develop coping strategies to deal with a panic attack during the attack and after it ends.

Coping Skills

Play games on IPAD	Take space	Count to 10	Think about happy memories	Talk to a friend
Talk to Mom or Dad	Stress balls	Play cards	Dance	Take a bath or shower
Excerise	Drawing	FREE SPACE!	Write in a journal	Arts and Crafts
Watch TV	Help a friend	Painting	Think about loved ones	Watch a movie
Take a walk	Deep breathing	Listen to music	Read	Go outside

And finally, create your calm down box similar to the one below and fill it with things you love and enjoy that help you calm

40 Ideas for the Perfect
CALM DOWN BOX

Something to Fidget
- Pipe Cleaners
- Nuts and Bolts
- Plastic Key Rings
- Cut up Pool Noodles
- Pom Poms

Something to Listen to
- Audio Book
- Calming Music
- NOTHING
- Noise Reducing Ear Muffs
- Affirmations

Something to Smell
- Cedarwood Essential Oil
- Lavender Scented Rice Bag
- Frankinsence Scented Felt
- Scented Playdough
- Fresh Flowers

Something to Look At
- Maze Book
- Kaleidoscope
- Glitter Jar
- Sand Timer
- Visual Reminders

Something to Squeeze
- Playdough Stress Ball
- Home made Weighted Lap Pad
- Stuffed Animal
- Pillow
- Putty

Something to Chew
- Chewable Jewelry
- Water Bottle
- Gum
- Clear Plastic Tubing
- Vibrating Toothbrush

down.

CALM DOWN BOX

Something to Fidget

Something to Listen To

Something to Smell

Something to Look At

Something to Squeeze

Something to Chew

3.5 Panic Attack Record Sheet and Crisis Plan

You can manage your life with panic disorder by keeping a record of your panic attacks. Writing is a simple and effective coping technique. You can monitor your development, examine your feelings, and reduce stress by keeping a record.

v

Panic Attack Worksheets by Inner Health Studio

What you were doing when it started?

What did you do during the panic attack?

What you were doing when the panic attack ended?

Did the panic attack begin suddenly or gradually? Did it end suddenly or gradually? How long did it take to go away?

What did you think was happening? When did you realize that this event was a panic attack?

Additional thoughts or comments:

Panic Attack Record Form

Date & Time	Fear rating (0-100%)

Situation	Trigger

Symptoms

- ☐ Heart pounding, racing, or palpitations
- ☐ Sweating
- ☐ Trembling or shaking
- ☐ Shortness of breath
- ☐ Feeling of choking
- ☐ Chest pain or discomfort
- ☐ Nausea or stomach distress
- ☐ Dizziness, lightheadedness, or feeling faint
- ☐ Chills or hot flushes
- ☐ Numbness or tingling
- ☐ Feelings of unreality
- ☐ Fear of losing control or going crazy
- ☐ Fear of dying

Thoughts (or Images)

Coping strategy

Finally, create a plan for the future when the panic attack hits so you can effectively cope with it!

Personal CRISIS PLAN

I know I'm triggered when I notice

_____
_____
_____

Some good ways to distract myself are:

SAFE People I can reach out to:

1. _____
2. _____
3. _____

Coping skills I can use:

Ways to keep myself & my space safe:

_____
_____
_____
_____

Other resources I can use to get Myself Care

1
2
3

Chapter 4: Stopping Negative Thinking and Unwanted Thoughts with CBT and Worksheets

A person usually has a lot of harmful self-statements and thoughts going through before they experience an unpleasant emotion, such as despair or anxiety. Such beliefs frequently follow a pattern, which is why we refer to them as problematic thinking styles.

4.1 Unhelpful Thinking

One of the things we observe is that people automatically adopt problematic thinking patterns; this is something we frequently fail to notice. Unfortunately, when someone uses some of these thinking patterns repeatedly and unceasingly, they often put themselves through significant emotional pain.

- **Jumping to conclusions**

When we presume that we know what another person is thinking (mind reading) and when we forecast what will happen in the future, we tend to jump to conclusions.

- **Black And White Thinking**

When thinking in this way, you only consider one extreme or the other. You are either right or wrong, good or evil, etc. There are no grey areas or shades of in-between.

- **Mental filtering**

This way of thinking includes filtering information in and out, creating a tunnel vision where one component of a scenario is focused on, and the rest is ignored.

This typically entails focusing on a scenario's bad aspects while ignoring its positive aspects, which can cause a single unpleasant detail to taint the entire situation.

- **Catastrophizing**

When we exaggerate problems and see them as terrible, awful, dreadful, and horrible, even though they are relatively minor, this is known as catastrophizing.

- **Emotional judgment**

This way of thinking entails basing your perception of events or yourself on how you feel. For instance, the fact that you feel as though something horrible is going to happen is the sole indication that it will.

- **Labeling**

When we create generalizations based on actions taken in certain circumstances, we label both ourselves and other people.

Even though numerous additional cases contradict this label, we may still use it.

Unhelpful Thinking

Unhelpful and negative thinking habits can lead to negative feelings without us even noticing. The first step in changing negative thoughts to more positive ones is to become more aware of what we think. Everyone has unhelpful thoughts sometimes but it's when they happen all of the time that they can have a negative impact on our mental health.
Which unhelpful thoughts do you recognise?

predictions
I will fail the test
I make negative predictions about what might happen in the future even though I have no way of knowing this.

judgements
They looked at me funny
I make judgements about things even though there is no evidence or facts to back this up.

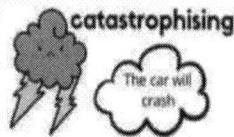

catastrophising
The car will crash
I always think that the worst thing or that something really bad is going to happen.

perfectionist
I have to get everything right
I put a lot of pressure on myself to do well and set unrealistically high expectations for myself.

negative glasses
Today has been terrible
When I have my negative glasses on, I only see the bad things and don't notice any of the good things.

feelings
I feel bad so that means today will be bad
If I notice negative feelings in myself or by body, I automatically think that it means something bad is happening.

mountains & molehills
I can't believe I only got 8 out of 10
I tend to take more notice of the negative things in a situation and down play the positive things.

memories
Something bad happened here so something bad will happen again
Some things trigger my negative memories which makes me think something bad will happen again now.

black & white thoughts
This day is ruined now
I usually think things are either really good or really bad with nothing in between.

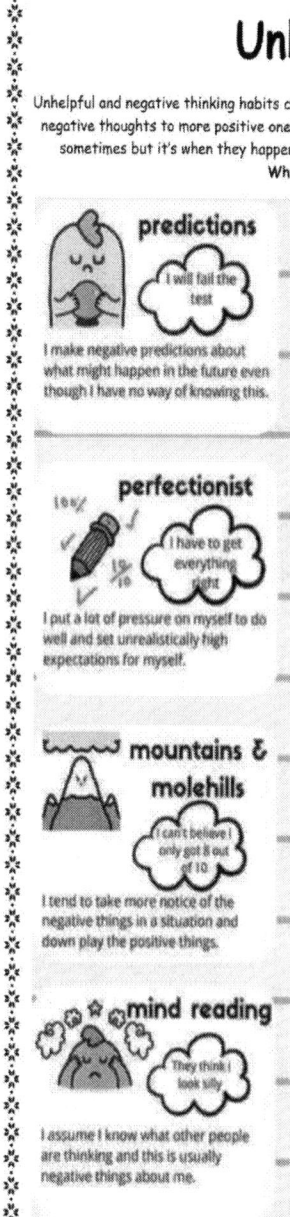

mind reading
They think I look silly
I assume I know what other people are thinking and this is usually negative things about me.

compare & despair
They are so clever, why can't I be like that?
I notice positive things about other people but then compare myself negatively to them.

self critical
I'm stupid
I am very critical of my own abilities and about myself.

4.2 Reality Acceptance Activities

When you reject reality, you become mired in unfavorable emotions like despair, rage, guilt, or bitterness. If you attempt to alter circumstances over which you have no control, you will also subject yourself to further misery. Whether we like it or not, certain things are just beyond our control. That is why it is essential to recognize false thoughts and state facts.

Reality Acceptance Worksheet

Realities that I am refusing to accept:

1. _____
2. _____
3. _____
4. _____
5. _____

Behaviors that I do when I am refusing to accept a reality (may look like a tantrum, giving up, manipulating, arguing, etc).

1. _____
2. _____
3. _____
4. _____
5. _____

How I experience SUFFERING when I refuse to accept reality:

1. _____
2. _____
3. _____
4. _____
5. _____

Are there any positives in me or the situation I am ignoring?

_____
_____
_____
_____
_____

Am I exaggerating how bad things will be?

_____
_____
_____
_____
_____
_____

4.3 Challenging Negative Thoughts Questionnaire

The method of reframing your negative self-talk to produce a positive shift in your mentality is known as challenging negative beliefs. However, it does require a little more work than simply attempting to think optimistically.

Challenging Negative Thoughts

Depression, poor self-esteem, and anxiety are often the result of irrational negative thoughts. Someone who regularly receives positive feedback at work might feel that they are horrible at their job because of one criticism. Their irrational thought about job performance will dictate how they feel about themselves. Challenging irrational thoughts can help us change them.

Answer the following questions to assess your thought:

Is there substantial evidence for my thought?

Is there evidence contrary to my thought?

Am I attempting to interpret this situation without all the evidence?

What would a friend think about this situation?

If I look at the situation positively, how is it different?

Will this matter a year from now? How about five years from now?

4.4 Brain Dump List

It is vital to empty your brain before lying down to get a good night's sleep without worries and wake up with a fresh mind. The best way to do so is by writing down your thoughts and concerns before you sleep and clearing the problems before you have them so you have nothing to worry about.

My Brain Dump List

- Procrastinations
- Fear
- Anger
- Discouragements
- Incomplete goals
- Sorrow

Nighttime Worries

I'm Worried About.....

_____

_____

_____

How Bad is it Really?

Not Bad ① ② ③ ④ ⑤ Really Bad

I Feel Anxious About.....

_____

_____

_____

How Bad is it Really?

Not Bad ① ② ③ ④ ⑤ Really Bad

I'm Concerned About....

_____

_____

_____

How Bad is it Really?

Not Bad ① ② ③ ④ ⑤ Really Bad

4.5 Self Affirmations

Your ability to change your negative thought patterns and transform them into positive ones is something that affirmations can help you with. They can also help you focus on achieving your life goals. According to research, it can keep us open to the thought that there is potential for development while reducing the tension, anxiety, and defensiveness linked to threats to our self-identity.

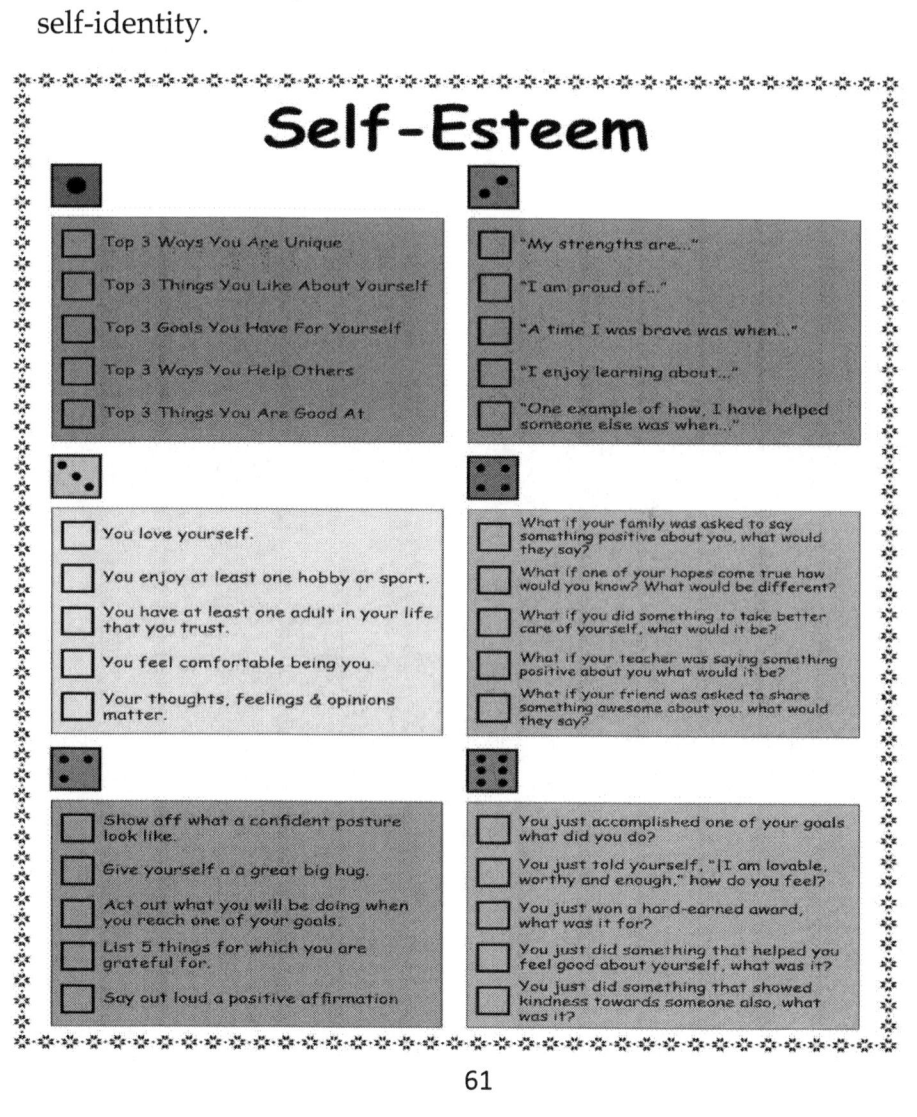

Self-Esteem

⚀
- [ ] Top 3 Ways You Are Unique
- [ ] Top 3 Things You Like About Yourself
- [ ] Top 3 Goals You Have For Yourself
- [ ] Top 3 Ways You Help Others
- [ ] Top 3 Things You Are Good At

⚁
- [ ] "My strengths are..."
- [ ] "I am proud of..."
- [ ] "A time I was brave was when..."
- [ ] "I enjoy learning about..."
- [ ] "One example of how I have helped someone else was when..."

⚂
- [ ] You love yourself.
- [ ] You enjoy at least one hobby or sport.
- [ ] You have at least one adult in your life that you trust.
- [ ] You feel comfortable being you.
- [ ] Your thoughts, feelings & opinions matter.

⚃
- [ ] What if your family was asked to say something positive about you, what would they say?
- [ ] What if one of your hopes come true how would you know? What would be different?
- [ ] What if you did something to take better care of yourself, what would it be?
- [ ] What if your teacher was saying something positive about you what would it be?
- [ ] What if your friend was asked to share something awesome about you, what would they say?

⚄
- [ ] Show off what a confident posture look like.
- [ ] Give yourself a a great big hug.
- [ ] Act out what you will be doing when you reach one of your goals.
- [ ] List 5 things for which you are grateful for.
- [ ] Say out loud a positive affirmation

⚅
- [ ] You just accomplished one of your goals what did you do?
- [ ] You just told yourself, "|I am lovable, worthy and enough," how do you feel?
- [ ] You just won a hard-earned award, what was it for?
- [ ] You just did something that helped you feel good about yourself, what was it?
- [ ] You just did something that showed kindness towards someone also, what was it?

Chapter 5: Activities to Stop Me from Feeling Anxious

It is crucial to challenge yourself regularly and move away from your comfort zone once in a while. These challenges are crucial for your well-being.

5.1 30-Day Anxiety Challenge

30 Day Anxiety Challenge

Make one anxiety goal for the next month.	Start exploring the root of any negative thoughts.	Work on a not good for you coping skill.	Build up your courage to face something you're avoiding.	Reach out to your support system about an anxious thought.
Change one thing in your day that will improve your anxiety	Check in with your anxiety goal and reevaluate.	Make sure your social media feeds are anxiety free.	Eat today in a way that feels good to body, mind, and soul.	Make a list of anxiety inducing things you're overcome.
Practice a new breathing technique.	Focus on sleep and rest and a healthy bedtime.	Make a list of three anxieties you want to work on.	Work on your self-talk, no mean words directed at yourself.	List your physical effects of anxiety. Work on one.
Work on going with the flow instead of resisting	List things you avoid because of your anxiety. Share it.	Create an emergency list for when your anxiety is high.	Do a full body scan. Where are you holding your anxiety?	What does your anxiety need from you today?
Spend 20 minutes listening to nature sounds.	Strengthen one of your coping skills by doing some research.	Practice mindfulness. Pull yourself back to the present.	Do something that helps you recharge where you feel drained.	Have self-compassion for yourself and your anxiety.
Go somewhere that relaxes you and eases anxiety.	Do a yoga routine on Youtube specifically for anxiety.	Read something that's good for your mental health.	Repair something that's been damaged by your anxiety.	Check in with your goal from day one. What's your progress?

This month, challenge yourself to beat anxiety and regain control of your life.

5.2 Anxiety Reduction Exercises

Check off every time you do these exercises. The more ticks there are, the closer you get to decreased anxiety.

1. Exercise in nature
2. Build up slowly - set & review goals
3. Find something you enjoy
4. Exercise with friends
5. Variety is the spice of life
6. Weekend boogie!
7. Strength training for mindfulness

5.3 I-Statements

Write one word daily from A-Z about the good qualities you find in yourself, starting with that letter to help you stop negative thinking.

My Positive Affirmations From A TO Z

Write out the positive affirmation(s) that best describe you!

I AM..

A _____	N _____
B _____	O _____
C _____	P _____
D _____	Q _____
E _____	R _____
F _____	S _____
G _____	T _____
H _____	U _____
I _____	V _____
J _____	W _____
K _____	X _____
L _____	Y _____
M _____	Z _____

5.4 Getting Over Negative Thinking Games and Activities

There are 42 negative thoughts. How many can you switch and change into positive thoughts? Put a cross on each box of the swirl ladder every time you are successfully able to change an opposing point of view into a positive one.

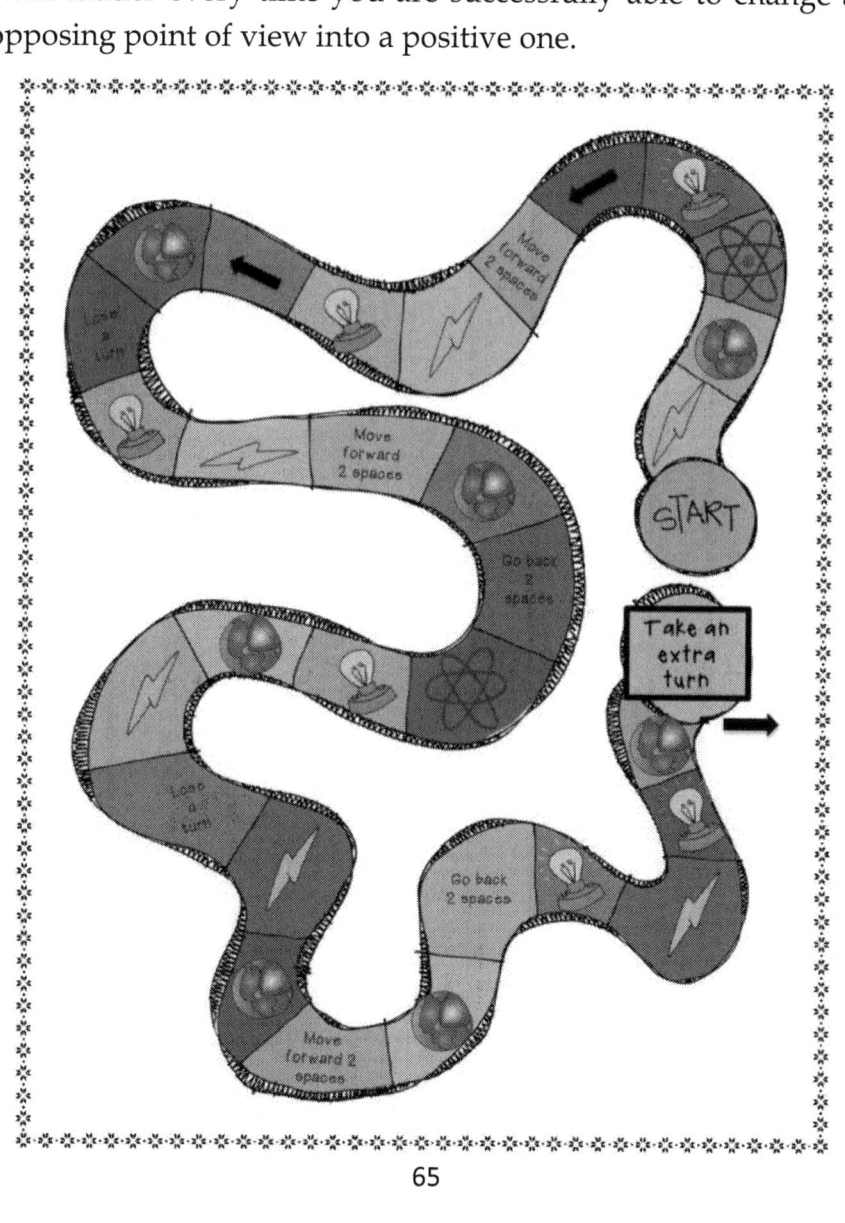

Negative thoughts	Positive thoughts	Negative thoughts	Positive thoughts
I am helpless, and I have no control		I'm so bored. There's nothing to do.	
I will lose		I hate those people. They make my life miserable.	
Nothing good ever happens to me.		I don't have what it takes to stick to a habit. I always give in.	
They don't love me		Everyone is annoying. No one matters	
I'm afraid I can't do this		I am worthless	
I will never lose all this weight.		I know there's something wrong with me.	
I'm not deserving and I'm not good enough.		I'll never be as successful as.	
I feel terrible, and I have no energy.		I am so ugly. Who would want to be with me?	
Why can't I be happy? I'm never happy.		I hate how my (face, hair, body, teeth, nose, etc.) looks.	
I can't stand that person. I am so angry.		I am a loser. I disgust myself.	
I'm getting so old, and I can't do anything anymore.		I had a bad childhood, so I'll never amount to much.	
I will never find love.		Nothing ever works out for me.	

Negative thoughts	Positive thoughts	Negative thoughts	Positive thoughts
I will never forgive them.		There's nothing I can do about it, so I'm giving up.	
I'll never make enough money.		What's the point of living?	
I'm overwhelmed. My life is a mess.		Why even bother? No one cares.	
I'm trapped in this situation and will never get out.		I'm too afraid. I can't do it.	
What if the worst happens? I know I'm jinxed.		If it weren't for ____. I would be happy.	
I'm sure I'll make a fool of myself.		It's not fair. I should be treated better.	
People are always out to get me.		I know I should do ____. But I have no motivation.	
Everything happening in the world is terrible.		My parents are disappointed in me; I am a failure.	
I'm a terrible person, and everyone can see it.		Why did I ever take this job? I hate it.	

5.5 How Do I Feel?

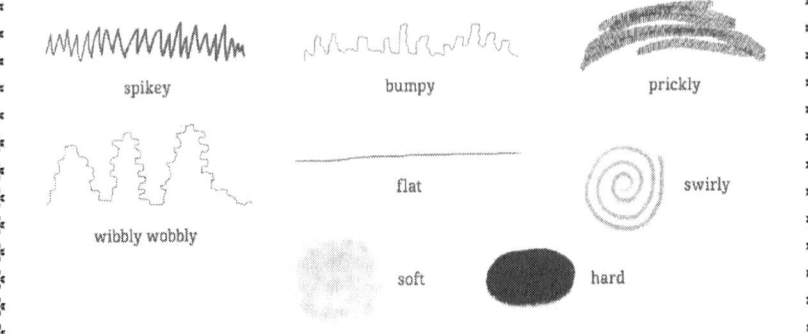

How Are You Feeling Today?

What color is your feeling?

Where do you feel this color in your body?

How BIG is your feeling?

Does it feel as BIG as a mountain?

Or does it feel middle-sized... like the size of a chair?

Or as small as a button?

If you could touch your feeling, how might it feel?

spikey

bumpy

prickly

wibbly wobbly

flat

swirly

soft

hard

What else would you like to say about your feeling?

5.6 Brain Dump Journal

Create a brain dump list with a pen when your mind begins to spiral into stress to help you release some of the mental tension.

The Brain Dump

Conclusion

When overwhelming feelings disrupt one's daily life, it is more than worry—it indicates anxiety. Teenagers with anxiety worry so much and frequently that it makes them uneasy. They are so concerned that if something terrible happens, it will be life-threatening and they have an extremely intense reaction like a panic attack. They start to let it interfere with their daily lives and find themselves skipping activities like using the elevator, taking a plane, or being late to class. These are brought on by such negative overthinking that is so intense that it makes you believe wrong things to be true. Because of their dread of injury, harmful, or even fatal outcomes, individuals quit performing simple tasks. You might have discovered various effective strategies for controlling your anxiety by completing the exercises in this book. Even while you will not ever experience anxiety again, you will have learned effective coping mechanisms that will allow you to live your life more quietly. No matter where you go or what you do for the rest of your life, you can keep your anxiety levels at a reduced level thanks to the new methods of thinking and acting that you have learned. Some people believe that since they have mastered these coping mechanisms, they should never experience anxiety again. They believe they must have done something wrong if they suffer the worry and their anxiety, anger, frustration, or depression increase. They believe their attempts to control their anxiousness have failed. It is crucial to remember that controlling anxiety and getting rid of it are two different things. Coping mechanisms assist you in taking care of yourself and preventing excessive anxiety. But coping mechanisms do not guarantee you will not ever experience anxiety again. Your life will constantly be filled with new difficulties and circumstances. It is impractical to anticipate total anxiety eradication. Thinking in this approach will make you feel like a failure because it is difficult to accomplish. The more you practice preventing and treating anxiety, the easier and faster it will be for you to deal with new situations when they come. But remember that you will encounter new difficulties that cause concern for the rest of your life. That only indicates that you are a living, breathing human being, not that you have failed.

Printed in Great Britain
by Amazon